My World

Diggers and Cranes

by Dr. Alvin Granowsky

Copper Beech Books
Brookfield, Connecticut

Contents

ON A BUILDING SITE   PAGE 4

BUILDING A ROAD   PAGE 18

© Aladdin Books Ltd 2000

Designed and produced by
Aladdin Books Ltd
28 Percy Street
London
W1P 0LD

Printed in Belgium
All rights reserved

Coordinator
Jim Pipe

First published in the
United States in 2000 by
Copper Beech Books,
an imprint of
The Millbrook Press
2 Old New Milford Road
Brookfield, Connecticut 06804

Design
Flick, Book Design and Graphics

Picture Research
Brian Hunter Smart

Library of Congress Cataloging-in-Publication Data

Granowsky, Alvin, 1936-
    Diggers and cranes / Alvin Granowsky.
    p. cm. -- (My world)
    ISBN 0-7613-1222-6 (lib. bdg.) ; 0-7613-2293-0 (paper ed.)
    1. Earthmoving machinery--Juvenile literature. 2. Cranes, derricks, etc.-- Juvenile
literature. [1. Earthmoving machinery. 2. Cranes, derricks, etc.] I. Title. II. My world
(Brookfield, Conn.)
TA725 .G72 2000
621.8'73--dc21   00-055597

Come one! Come all! Meet the diggers and cranes that make hard work seem easy.

Some are big, some are small. Some are short and some are tall.

These machines can dig, lift, push, and drill. Meet the diggers and cranes that get the big jobs done!

Diggers

A shovel and pail are great for work and play at the beach.

When you work on big buildings and big roads, it is diggers and cranes that you want.

Digger

Crane

Diggers are like giant shovels, and cranes are like giant pails, with the power to get big jobs done.

Look at those diggers and cranes at work on a building. They are great for getting big jobs done!

How many diggers can you see?

Building site

7

What if you just had a little hammer to knock down this old building? Bang, bang! This job could take forever.

Muncher

Now use this muncher. It grabs the walls with its jaws and takes a big bite. Crunch! Watch the walls fall down!

Jaws

Big digger

A big, wide hole needs to be dug for the bottom of a giant building. Do you grab your shovel and pail and start digging?

No! You hop into this digger and let it do the work for you.

Wow! Look at that digger scoop up the earth. That hole will be dug in no time at all!

Loading a truck

Drilling a hole

You need to dig a very deep hole.

Do you grab your shovel and start digging?

Stop! It will be better to use this drill.

Look at its sharp edges spin around and around, like a drill at home. With this machine you can dig a hole in no time!

Electric drill

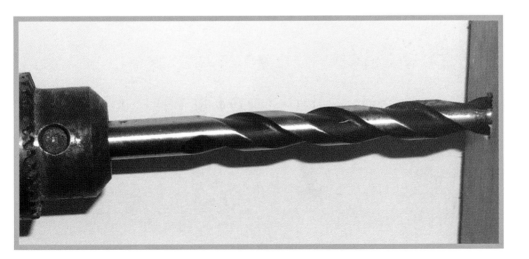

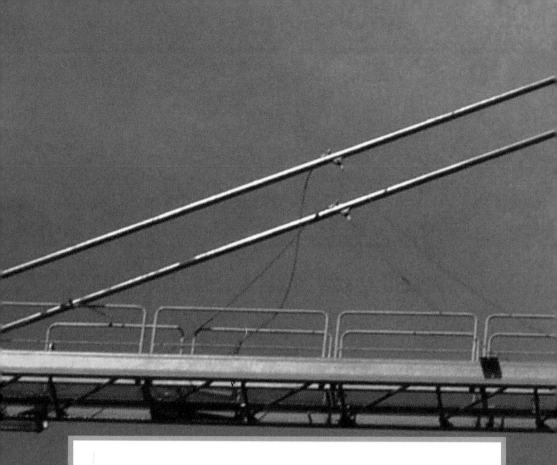

You need a load of bricks on the
top of that tall building. Do you
put the bricks in your pail and
start climbing? Stop! Let this tall
crane do the carrying for you.

Tower crane

15

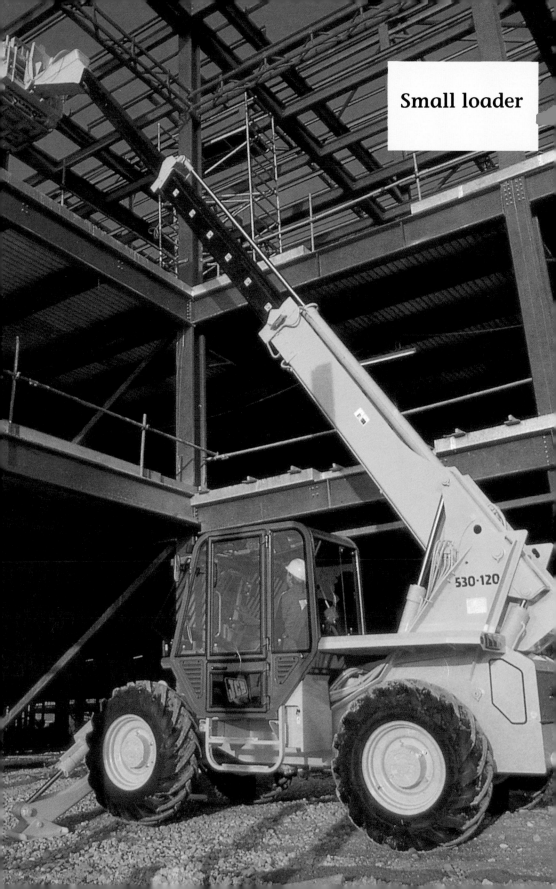

Small loader

This space is too small for a big crane to fit.
It is too small for a big digger too.

How can this job be done?
Small loaders and little diggers
will work in small places.

Small digger

You are building a big road.
Do you run to get your shovel
and pail? No. Use these
big machines instead!

Building a road

19

You have a huge pile of earth to move.
What do you do? Use this bulldozer!
A bulldozer is great for pushing
earth out of the way.

Bulldozer

Scraper

Oh, no! There are bumps in the road!

Don't worry. This digger will scrape

away the bumps for you.

That is why it is called a scraper.

Can you lift this huge pipe?
With this strong crane, you can
lift the pipe easily.

Crawler cranes

Guess what this crane is called. It's a crawler crane because it crawls across the ground.

23

How would you like to drive this digger? It can do a lot of jobs.

Do-it-all digger

It hammers.

It moves earth.

It digs holes.

It makes the ground flat.

There are diggers for all types of jobs.

This big one is made to dig rocks from the ground. Would you like to drive this digger someday?

Mining shovel

Can You Find?

Some diggers have wheels, others have tracks. It is easy for a digger or crane with tracks to move across bumpy ground.

Tracks

Look for these wheels and tracks—what machines are they on? *Clue:* Look at pages 16, 17, 20, 24, and 29.

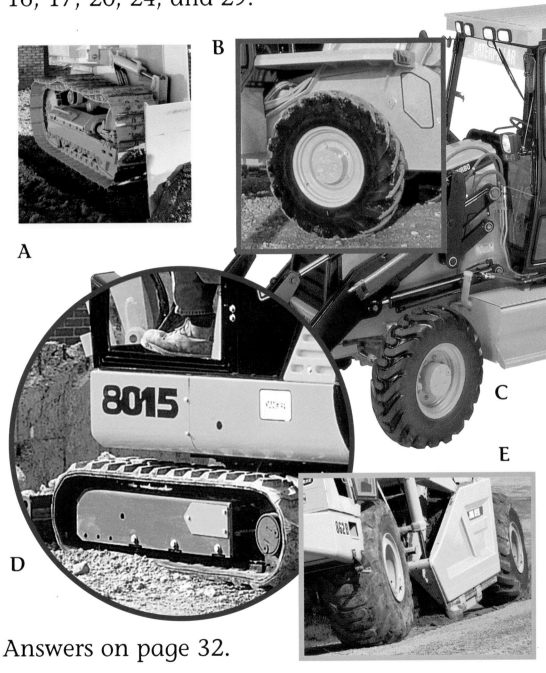

A

B

C

D

8015

E

8620

Answers on page 32.

Do You Know?

Not all diggers move earth.

Can you tell what these diggers are doing?

A

B

C

Can you match each machine below to its job? The answers are on page 32.

1

Lifting

2

Pushing

3

Digging

Index

ANSWERS TO QUESTIONS

Page 29 – **A** comes from the bulldozer.
• **B** comes from the small loader • **C** comes from
the do-it-all digger • **D** comes from the small digger.
• Wheel **E** is from the scraper.

Page 30 – Digger **A** is clearing trees in a forest.
• Digger **B** is clearing snow from a road.
• Digger **C** is working on a farm.

Page 31 – **1** is a digger, built for digging.
• **2** is a crane, built for lifting.
• **3** is a bulldozer, built for pushing earth.